KNOW THYSELF

A Guided Journal

For Those Beginning the Journey of Self-Knowledge

By Laura E. Wolfe and
Leah M. Sommers

KNOW THYSELF: A Guided Journal

Copyright © **2019 Leah M. Sommers and Laura E. Wolfe**

All rights reserved.

Published by **Kindle Direct Publishing 2018**

Pennsylvania, United States

No parts of this publication may be reproduced, stored in a retrieval system, or transmitted in any form or by any means, electronic, mechanical, photocopying, recording, or otherwise, without the prior written permission of the copyright owner.

This book is sold subject to the condition that it shall not, by way of trade or otherwise, be lent, resold, hired out, or otherwise circulated without the publisher's prior consent in any form of binding or cover other than that in which it is published and without a similar condition including this condition being imposed on the subsequent purchaser. Under no circumstances may any part of this book be photocopied for resale.

Cover Image Created by Freepik

For All Fellow Adventurers

Table of Contents

Introduction 7

Chapter One: Begin at the Beginning 13

Chpater Two: Personality Inventory 32

Chapter Three: Emotional Inventory 51

    "Plutchik-wheel" *54*

Chapter Four: Ego Structure and the False Self 76

Chapter Five: Mind/Body/Spirit Inventory 92

Chapter Six: Biology and Society 110

Chapter Seven: Cognitive Dissonance 125

Chapter Eight: Values and Character 146

    Virtue *150*

Chapter Nine: I and Thou 164

Chapter Ten: Autobiography, Autopsychotherapy, Autointellectus 180

Appendix 1: Detailed Wheel of Emotions 184

Appendix 2: Table of Virtues 185

Further Resources 186

Influences 188

Introduction

There is an entire universe within you. As a wise monk once said, "The heart is a small vessel, and yet dragons are there, lions are there... there is also God, the angels, life and light."

But how do you find your way into that world? It seems to come so naturally to some people—they speak of inner dialogues and levels of consciousness in ways that seem like magic. For many, the inner world would be more accessible if it planted itself on Antarctica.

You can imagine your inner world like the submerged portion of an iceberg. The tip visible above water is your conscious life— the thoughts that cloud around you like buzzing flies, your plans and reactions to the physical world around you. The mountain beneath is the rest of who you are. If you were a machine, this is where you would store your directives: the operating principles that help you make decisions according to your priorities. We all have priorities, whether we've deliberately chosen them or not. Excavating the iceberg is part of the process of figuring out just what has been running our lives.

Another useful picture is the idea of the subconscious as the basement of your mind. If you've ever lived in one place for a long time, you know how places like the basement gradually fill up with the accumulated detritus of the years. You can ignore the fact that your basement is a mess—but ignoring the mess won't get rid of it! And the funny thing about cluttered basements is that those are the ones with spooky, shadowed corners. If a monster was going to hide somewhere, you know instinctively which corner it would pick. Cleaning out the basement is another part of the process of figuring out what fears are hiding underneath layers of more rational, "grown-up" thoughts.

Icebergs and basements—they don't necessarily make this inner world sound very pleasant or safe. So why would you want to go there?

Well, for one, because it's an adventure. And not just any old adventure—this is the unique adventure of your life. No one else contains the same jumble of mysteries. Only you. In a sense, this adventure is what you were made for.

Self-knowledge, the process of going within, is not easy. Courageously facing the truth about ourselves, deliberately choosing to become involved in our own creation—these are heroic actions. And as Lao Tzu said, "A journey of a thousand miles begins with a single step."

Now for the disclaimer. We are not trained professionals, and this book is no substitute for professional care from the right person. We are regular people who have spent decades on this journey, and are planning to continue on until our final breaths. But one of the things we've noticed is that people we love want to start their own adventures and are stuck at obstacles we recognize. We would like to offer the following guide in the spirit of help from fellow adventurers.

Many of us had childhoods that lacked in one way or another, and we are in the position of needing to gain essential life-and-growth navigation skills on our own, or with the help of others. Usually part of doing this involves revisiting important memories from our lives, and reflecting on how they impacted us, what we learned, and how we might now understand them differently, or relate differently to the feelings they evoke. It is at the place of these painful memories that we often remain stuck, even if time has gone on and many years have passed.

Of course, how you have spent the ensuing years matters a great deal both to who you are now and to how you will understand your past! Affirming value wherever you find it is just as important as excavating uncomfortable memories— like unpacking a forgotten box of old Christmas ornaments and hanging them up instead of just determinedly cleaning out the clutter. From this very hour, from this very minute, living according to the values you deliberately choose strengthens and shapes who you are, regardless of how much conscious introspection you do.

Something that is very exciting to realize is that all meaning has context. Nothing has meaning in isolation, but rather the connections to other things and events give them relevance and story. The overall narrative of your life is being continually shaped, moment by moment, by your ongoing experiences and choices. You can change the meaning of your past by changing the trajectory of your story—a tragedy in act one becomes redemption in act three, for example. This means that by changing who you are now, in a very real sense *you can change the past itself.*

Sometimes our experience has led us to use certain vocabulary from different schools of psychology or philosophical thought, and included in the back is an appendix of resources that we have found helpful or thought-provoking. While we have found different models to be helpful at different stages of our journeys, that doesn't mean that the same thoughts will be as useful to you as they were to us. Our best advice here is this: Take what is useful to you, discard what is not.

Some Words of Caution

"Ego" is a technical term that gets used in many different ways at the vernacular level. Often, the process of introspection helps you to figure out the differences between your ego and your self, a distinction that at first encounter can feel intimidating and impossible. One of the ways to think about ego is as a personality structure that evolves in response to, and in collaboration with, your instinctual feelings, responses, emotions, and drives on the one hand and the expectations of your social environment on the other. It is part of who you are: part of the surface of the iceberg, if you will, and not necessarily a bad thing. Ideally, a strong, flexible ego will develop that is adapted to and meaningfully engaged with the external world and that is also in a state of honest, aware connection to the world within.

Sometimes this process of development goes awry and the necessity for adaptation becomes problematic in one way or another. Excellent parenting will involve modeling to a child how to effectively deal with their emotions (in a socially responsible way) and also how to live life with values— from the large picture to the small details. Of course, not all of us had the benefits of excellent parenting, even when our parents were well-meaning, benevolent people who did the best that they were able to do.

There is no way around it; introspection involves exhuming the past and uncovering hidden parts of ourselves that can make us uncomfortable, to say the least. Sometimes confronting past memories or painful, confusing feelings can be both scary and overwhelming. If your "ego-self-structure" is currently somewhat weak, it is even liable to being "flooded" by this painful backlog of emotion. This can make you feel destabilized—or even literally destabilize you with physical symptoms. When this happens, it's important to keep some perspective on all the things that matter.

Exploring your inner world is important, but so is the beautiful, priceless, and irreplaceable life you live now. If your "growth process" starts to feel too intense or overwhelming, by all means dial it back a bit! Remember, your goal is to grow and develop, not to destroy yourself. Don't be afraid to push yourself a little, but realize that you need balance, and that's okay.

Another thing that is important to keep in mind in the journey of self-discovery and development is perspective. It can be very helpful and reassuring, even soothing, to bounce things off another person and benefit from their perspective— i.e., the different context of understanding their experiences and personality provide. On our journeys we have found this benefit in close friends and loved ones as well as in psychological professionals. However, when we are vulnerable it can be too easy to idealize another person that we see as having it more together than ourselves, and this idealization can often lead to disappointment, pain, and confusion of its own. This is another aspect of the journey that requires caution, mindfulness, and taking things slowly.

None of this is an overnight process; it is the never-ending work of a lifetime. However, seeing yourself as on a journey of growth and discovery versus merely struggling to get through the days and meet obligations can make all the difference in the world.

Remember, this is an adventure! In that venturesome spirit, we offer you this hand-sketched map, if you will, for engaging your inner and outer worlds with more gusto, excitement and purpose. Be good to yourself and know this: you are ultimately on the side of worth and meaning, of the pricelessness of life. The fact that you took up this book is evidence of the value you see in yourself, and in every step you take in life, the things you notice, the words you say, the things you do, you have another chance to affirm value where you see it.   Bon voyage!

"One can have no smaller or greater mastery than mastery of oneself."

- Leonardo da Vinci

Chapter One:
Begin at the Beginning

1. If your life was a story or a play, how would it be divided? Name and list the eras, acts, or chapters of your life.

> *Examples*: Early Childhood/Before Parents' Divorce; Childhood After Parents' Divorce; Puberty through High School; College; Career Path; Marriage; Parenthood; Before and After a Significant Death, etc.

2. Describe your personality as a young child, at any prepubescent age that feels accessible to you. What did it feel like to be you?

3. Thinking about yourself as a child, what was your typical energy level like? Did you need to move a lot?

4. As a young child, what were you curious about? Did you ask many questions? Who did you ask, and what sorts of things did you ask about?

5. Thinking about your five senses, try to recall a memory or two strongly associated with each sense (i.e., the smell of Thanksgiving dinner, the colors in a favorite piece of clothing, the feel of a pet). They can be positive or negative memories, or even both!

    Visual/Sight

    Auditory/Hearing

Olfactory/Smell

Gustatory/Taste

Tactile/Touch

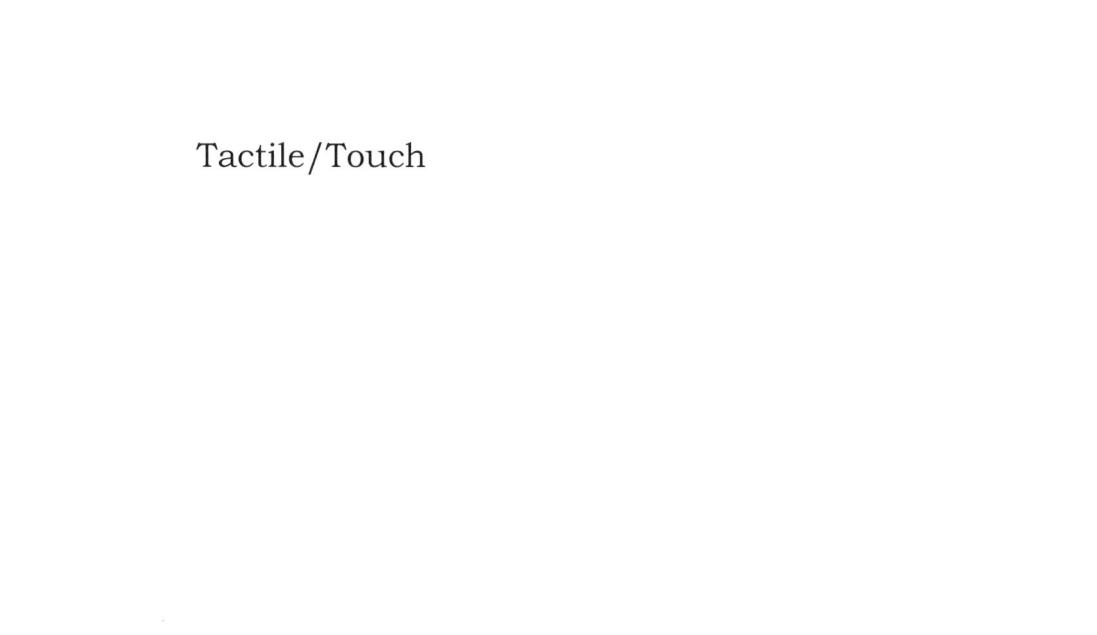

Which sense has the most powerful memories?

6. Describe some of your favorite daydreams as a child.

7. What was your relationship like with each of your parents? What did you do together, what did you talk about, if anything?

8. Did you have any other important adults in your life— relatives, neighbors or friends? Who were they and what were your relationships with them like?

9. What were your ideas of right and wrong like as a child?

10. Tell about a memory from your early childhood. What were you feeling at the time? Now imagine yourself as an adult in the room. What would you see? What context could you give the child?

11. Describe one or more content, peaceful memories from your childhood. If that child could speak to you, what would he or she tell you? How can you bring the lessons of those moments forward into the present?

12. Describe one or more painful experiences from your childhood. Knowing what you know now, what would you like to tell the suffering child? If there were others involved in the memory, what do you wish they had understood about that child? How would you parent that child, knowing what you know about the child's pain?

13. Repeat questions 10, 11 and 12 as necessary, for as many memories as you wish. The more you examine, the greater your understanding of your younger self will be.

14. Recall a time in your childhood where you felt abandoned.

15. Do you have any noticeable or unusually large gaps in your memory? List them.

16. Meditate on the eras or chapter headings of your life that you listed in the first question. Without going into detail, list underneath each heading any major life lessons learned in each era.

Chapter Two: Personality Inventory

1. Would you describe yourself as introverted, extroverted or both? Why?

2. Describe your current fantasy life.

3. How important is artistic creativity to you?

4. How do you experience poetry, dance, music, or art?

5. How do you experience math and logic?

6. How do you perceive your environment, the world around you?

7. Does your environment affect your state of mind?

8. Would you describe yourself as aggressive, passive or assertive? Why?

9. Describe your inner life—thoughts, dreams, stories you tell yourself about yourself, etc.

10. How do you share this experience with others?

11. Do your thoughts happen to you, or do you make your own thoughts?

12. How would you describe the level of control you have over your thoughts?

13. Describe a time when thoughts seemed to be something that came to you from outside yourself. How did you handle that situation?

14. Have you ever taken any kind personality quiz? Did you think the assessment described you accurately? Did you disagree with anything?

15. Recall a time when you experienced guilt. What did you do about it?

16. Recall a time when you made someone else feel guilty. What came of it?

17. Tell about a recent time where you did not like a person. What didn't you like about them and why?

18. Have you ever thought or behaved in a similar way to the person in the above question? How and why?

Chapter Three: Emotional Inventory

1. Imagine a pressure gauge that measures the intensity of your emotion. How intense do your emotions feel on a typical day? On a particularly good day? On a particularly bad day?

2. Describe your own personal extremes of emotion.

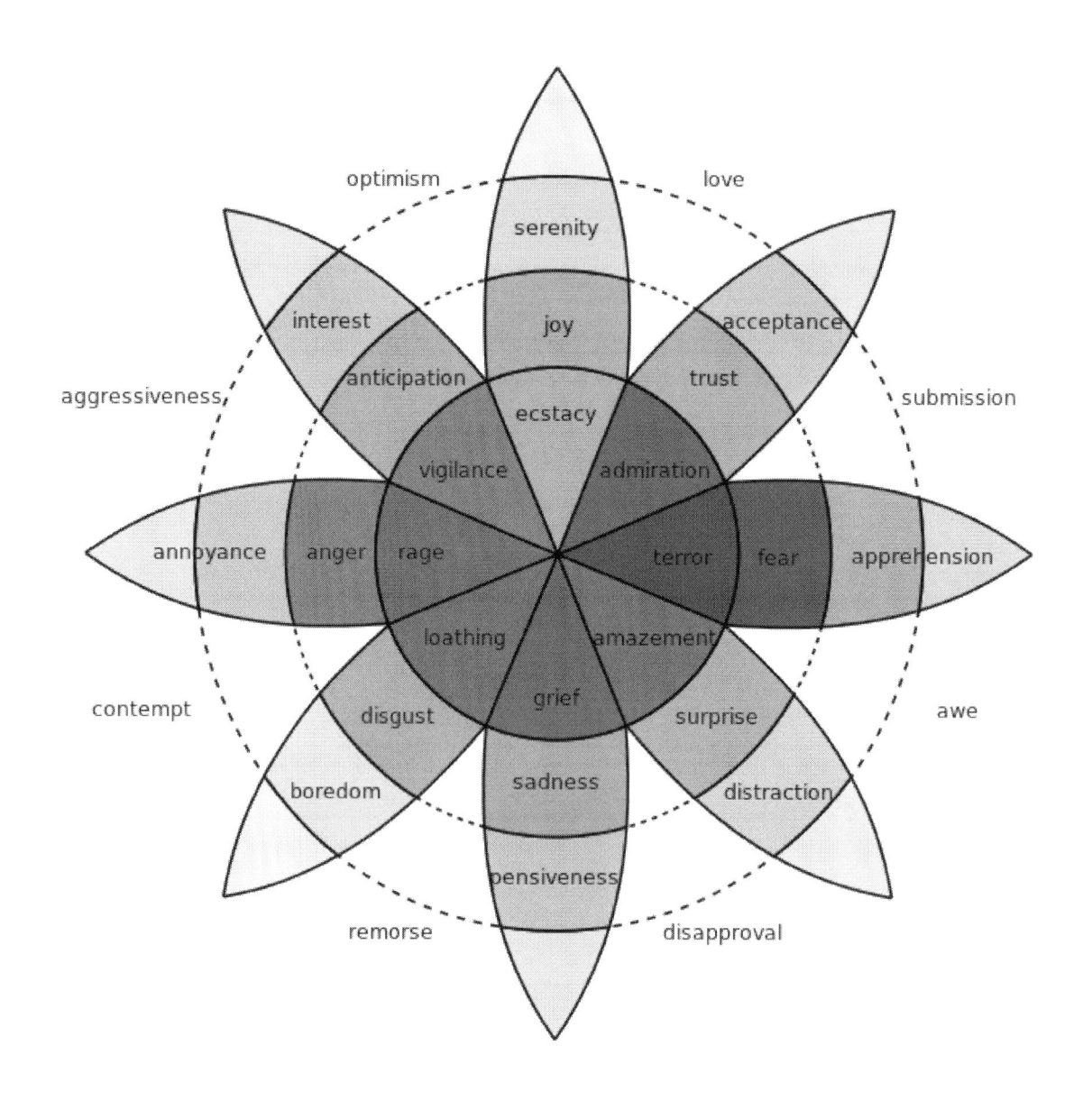

"Plutchik-wheel" by Machine Elf 1735 - Own work. Licensed under Public Domain via Wikimedia Commons - http://commons.wikimedia.org/wiki/File:Plutchik-wheel.svg#mediaviewer/File:Plutchik-wheel.svg

Note: For a more detailed wheel of emotions, see appendix.

3. Think about the relative intensity of your emotions. Which emotions do you experience most intensely? (See Plutchik's Wheel of Emotions for ideas.)

4. Which emotions do you experience mildly? (See Plutchik's Wheel of Emotions for ideas.)

5. Describe the way your body feels for each of your emotions.

6. What emotions do you have a hard time dealing with?

7. Which ones make you feel unsafe, or unable to handle them? Which ones make you feel like you have lost control?

8. What emotions do you associate with being a successful person?

9. What emotions make you feel like you are in control of yourself?

10. Empathy is the ability to experience the feelings of another person. Describe your sense of empathy. Tell about a time where you experienced empathy with another person.

11. Sympathy is the feeling of care, understanding, or compassion for another person. Describe your sense of sympathy. Tell about a different time when you experienced sympathy.

12. Do you consider your emotions to be linked to your physical health? That is, do you think emotions indicate something about your body's condition?

13. Does the state of your body cause emotions, or do emotions cause changes in your body?

14. Do you consider your emotions to be linked to your spiritual self? That is, do you think your emotions indicate something about your spiritual state?

15. Does the state of your spirit cause emotions, or do emotions cause changes in your spirit?

16. Do you wish you could stop experiencing any of your emotions? Why? What would be the benefit?

17. Do you believe any of your emotions are "bad"? How would a change in your emotion make you a better or worse person?

18. What are emotions good for? How do you use your emotions to inform your life?

19. How do you feel when you have to deal with the negative emotions of other people?

20. Tell about a time you had to deal with a person who was angry or critical.

21. Tell about a time you had to comfort someone who was sad or depressed.

22. Have you ever felt intoxicated by an emotion? Describe the experience.

23. Have you ever felt numb, or completely blank of emotion? Describe the experience.

Chapter Four:
Ego Structure and the False Self

1. Who are you? Answer this question using a free-write technique: For ten minutes, write whatever comes to your mind.

2. What roles do you have? List as many as you can.

3. Rank your roles in order of their importance to you.

4. Describe the self you need to be in order to fulfill a specific role. (i.e. "In order to be a good employee, I have to be…") Do this for at least the first three roles in your list; however, the more roles you examine, the greater your understanding will be.

5. In the roles you have outlined, highlight and list the qualities that feel like they are not a part of the true you.

6. Do those qualities serve a helpful function in the role you must play?

7. Does practicing those qualities cause you to feel a sense of betrayal to yourself?

8. Recall a time when you felt like a victim of uncontrollable circumstances. What did you do about it?

9. List any and all groups and/or tribes of which you consider yourself a member. Include consumer/product/lifestyle groups as well as political or religious affiliations.

10. Rank the groups in the previous list according to their importance to you. Why are the top three groups important to you?

11. How does membership in one of these groups affirm who you feel you really are? What does membership mean about what kind of person you are?

12. Imagine not being part of a group or tribe. How would that change your opinion of yourself?

13. Is it possible to identify as a member of a group and not feel like it is part of who you truly are? Is this a good thing or a bad thing? Why?

14. What skills do you have that allow you to engage in your groups of choice in ways that you find pleasant?

15. How do you feel when one of your chosen groups thinks or behaves in ways that you disagree with?

Chapter Five:
Mind/Body/Spirit Inventory

1. Describe your diet over the course of a week.

2. What is your current sleep schedule?

3. What is your current exercise regime?

3. How much alcohol do you consume on a weekly basis? Other recreational drugs?

4. Do you have any issues with pain or illness? What are they?

5. If you have health issues, imagine what your life would be like if they were gone. What would it be like? What would be different?

6. What are you willing to do in order to feel healthy and strong?

7. What are you not willing to change, regardless of whether or not it would improve your life?

8. For one day, write down every stray thought that crosses your mind. Do not think about your thoughts, just write them down.

9. When you observe your thoughts, do you notice more words with negative meanings or more words with positive meanings?

10. Do you pray every day? Why or why not?

11. What prayers do you use, if any? Why?

12. What do you want to get out of prayer?

13. Do you meditate every day? Why or why not?

14. Do you use a specific technique or mantra? Why or why not?

15. What do you want to get out of meditation?

16. Describe your ideal mind/body/spirit health schedule. Include food, exercise, sleep, work, creative activities and spiritual activities such as prayer and meditation.

Chapter Six:
Biology and Society

1. Think of a time in your life when you did what was expected of you, by society, your family or your peers, without reflection. How did it feel at the time? How do you feel about it now?

2. When have you accepted the thought processes of others because you liked the way they sounded or felt? Or because they made you feel intelligent or accomplished?

3. Do you eat what you want, when you want it? Why or why not?

4. When sexual arousal occurs, do you feel entitled to resolve the arousal with a sexual experience (with others or alone)?

5. Take a moment to imagine a very successful person. Describe their lifestyle, their choices, their public history. Come up with a few interesting tidbits about this successful person.

6. Think of the successful person from the last question. Now describe their character.

7. Which description was easier, 5 or 6? Why?

8. Was your successful person wealthy? Why or why not? Were they physically attractive? Why or why not?

9. What does success mean to you?

10. Biological drives include the need or desire for food, water, sleep, sex, or relief of pain or boredom. Describe a time when you made a decision based primarily off of a biological drive or reason. How did you feel about the decision at the time? How do you feel now?

11. Societal norms are expectations we have internalized because "everyone" does it. Describe a time when you made a decision based primarily on conforming to a societal norm. How did you feel about the decision at the time? How do you feel now?

12. Think of the earliest time when you did not like yourself. Tell the story.

13. Tell about a time you sought someone's approval and felt like you were betraying yourself in the process.

14. Tell about a time you isolated yourself from others in order to protect yourself from the possibility of displeasing another person.

Chapter Seven:
Cognitive Dissonance

1. Describe your personality as an early teenager.

2. Tell about a time during your adolescence when you first were offended by the hypocrisy of adults.

3. How did you want them to behave then? Looking back on it now, if you could make them behave in a certain way, how would you have them behave?

4. In those behaviors you preferred, why are they more satisfying? What is good about them? What do you perceive as better than how the person in question really behaved?

5. Describe a time when you felt like society wanted you to act like a robot.

6. Describe a time when you felt dehumanized.

7. Describe how you think others see you.

8. How do you relate to authority in others?

9. How do you act when you are an authority?

10. Describe a time when you acted in a way that you felt was not true to yourself.

11. What would you change about how you handled the situation?

12. Tell about a time when as an adult, you were offended by the double standards of a manager or boss.

13. How should they have behaved? Why?

14. How would you have behaved in a similar situation? Why?

15. In those behaviors you preferred, why are they more satisfying? What is good about them? What do you perceive as better than how the person in question really behaved?

16. Describe a time when you felt a distinct difference between reality as–it-is and reality as how it could be, if it were better.

17. Describe your ideal personality.

18. Describe your anxieties, insecurities, and times of depression.

19. How have your experiences with anxiety, insecurity and depression informed your personality?

20. Imagine yourself without any history of anxiety, insecurity, depression, physical illness, or spiritual doubt. Would your life be better or worse? Why?

Chapter Eight: Values and Character

1. Describe how you think others see you.

2. How do you want others to see you?

3. Think of a recent experience and retell that experience from the perspective of another person involved.

Virtue

Note: If the graphic is difficult to read, please see table in appendix.

4. Some people's bodies are naturally suited to baseball, swimming, bodybuilding, etc. Some people have to work harder than others to grow and train the correct muscles. Which virtues come naturally to you? Which are difficult?

5. List ten character virtues that you want to form the bedrock of your personality.

6. What can you do to strengthen those virtues?

7. List three virtues that do not come easily to you. What can you do to incorporate practicing them into your daily life?

8. Think of yourself in a bad mood. What sorts of things can put you in a bad mood?

9. What are your emotions like in a bad mood?

10. What good qualities become especially difficult for you when you are under duress? How does a bad mood affect your ability to engage in virtue?

11. What are your typical coping mechanisms for dealing with bad moods? What else would you like to try?

12. Can you control your moods? Why or why not?

13. Imagine yourself in 90 days. How would you like to be different within that time frame?

14. Recall the past 90 days. How have you changed, for better or for worse, within that time frame?

15. Think of a person or character that you admire. What about them is essential—that is, if you took it away, they would be less than what they are?

16. Imagine your admired person completing an exercise such as this journal. What sorts of things do you imagine that they say to themselves or about themselves?

Chapter Nine: I and Thou

1. Immanuel Kant described the most important rule, his "categorical imperative" in this way: Never treat a person as a means to an end, but always as an end in and of themselves. Describe a time when you felt treated as a means to an end by someone else.

2. Describe a time when you felt treated like an "end in itself"; that is, when your interactions with someone felt like they were completely altruistic in intention towards you.

3. Describe a time when you treated another person as a means to an end. How do you feel about it on reflection?

4. Describe an encounter when you felt fully present with another person, and had no motive other than to listen to them and enjoy being with them.

5. Describe a time when you were aware of another person only as you experienced them—that is, when you noticed and catalogued details about their physical appearance, mannerisms, or context.

6. Think about the words *behold* and *encounter*. Describe a time when your interactions with another person felt like these words.

7. Think of the word *participate*. Describe a relationship where the other person feels like part of your very self—to know them or love them is to be more of who you really are.

8. Think of a relationship that you have that you would like to develop. How could your experience of that person change?

9. What could a meaningful *encounter* with that person be like? What could it be like to *behold* that person?

10. What could it be like if you were able to participate in each other's being?

11. What is the purpose of relationships?

12. How could *beholding* someone else change how you see yourself?

13. Consider *beholding* an inanimate creature or object, such as a tree or a rock. How might that be different from just experiencing these things? What might it be like to *participate* with them? How might it change the way you see yourself?

14. Can you have an *encounter* with God, as you understand Him? Why or why not? What might that be like?

15. *Behold* yourself. How would you describe your relationship with yourself, within yourself? What would you like that *encounter* to be like?

Chapter Ten: Autobiography, Autopsychotherapy, and Autointellectus

Tell your story, analyze your narrative, understand yourself

One of the most basic and important tools you can create to foster self-understanding is your own autobiography. This story that you tell, however, cannot be the wishful fiction that comes to the unexamined mind and heart.

Before you sit down to write your story, take the time to create a writing ritual. Make a cup of coffee or tea, dress comfortably, find a welcoming corner of your home or a little café and settle in with a computer or pen and paper. Imagine yourself confiding in the most understanding, trustworthy friend in the whole world. This person will not misunderstand you, no matter how clumsily you word something, and this person will always give you the benefit of the doubt. This person wishes you nothing but peace and joy and will do anything to help you.

Flip back to chapter one of this book. Using the chapter headings you created in the first question, begin to write the story of your life. Tell what happened, describe what you were feeling. Judge whomever you wish. Explain yourself in detail. Use the questions from this book to prompt your thoughts, and look over your answers with a new eye. Dive down any rabbit hole that catches your attention.

When you have naturally finished a section, or a portion of a section, set aside your writing for a period of time. Take an hour, maybe a day, perhaps a week to clear your mind. When you return to your writing, imagine yourself as sitting down for a cup of tea with a beloved, cherished friend whom you have missed. Someone with whom you feel absolutely safe.

Now imagine that you have reversed the roles. You are the cherished friend and you are going to read what your friend has written about their life. Imagine that what you are reading about happened to another person. Listen with compassion. Take notes on your reactions, thoughts and feelings. Tell your story itself how you feel about reading it.

You are the speaker and the listener. Ask yourself questions. Explain things that are unclear. Wrestle with the things you do not understand. Try on different explanations, offered to yourself the way you might offer advice to a respected friend. Give yourself pushback, but be gentle and loving. You are the counselor and the counseled, and no one can corrupt the self-understanding that you discover.

Pay attention to your painful experiences. What do you want your suffering self to know or to learn from them?

Note throughout your story that you are capable of love, joy and peace. How can you recreate those experiences or feelings today?

There are plenty of variations and enrichments to the activity of writing your story. One way is to play with creativity in the context of your story. As you reflect on details of your past or the memory of a significant event, think about some of the wider things going on— positive things alongside with pain, light with dark, and the ever-present beauty of the natural world surrounding you with a constant benediction. When you are ready, reflect on those as well. Pull out some paints or sketch pad. Doodle your thoughts or color them, and don't self-censor—let things flow. If you are musically inclined, sing or play some music that reflects your mood and state of mind. Afterwards, have a snack or a cup of coffee, or go for a walk. Maybe spend some time in prayer and meditation.

Most of all, remember that this process takes time. Be patient and gentle with yourself, and take breaks when you need them. Be cautious of allowing the past to take over the importance of the present. Whatever you learn in your autobiography has already happened, but tomorrow has not. Make small, healthy decisions and reasonable changes of habit. Look forward to the future, but don't live there. It is in the heart where eternity touches the present and peace is possible. We wish you joy.

Appendix 1: Detailed Wheel of Emotions

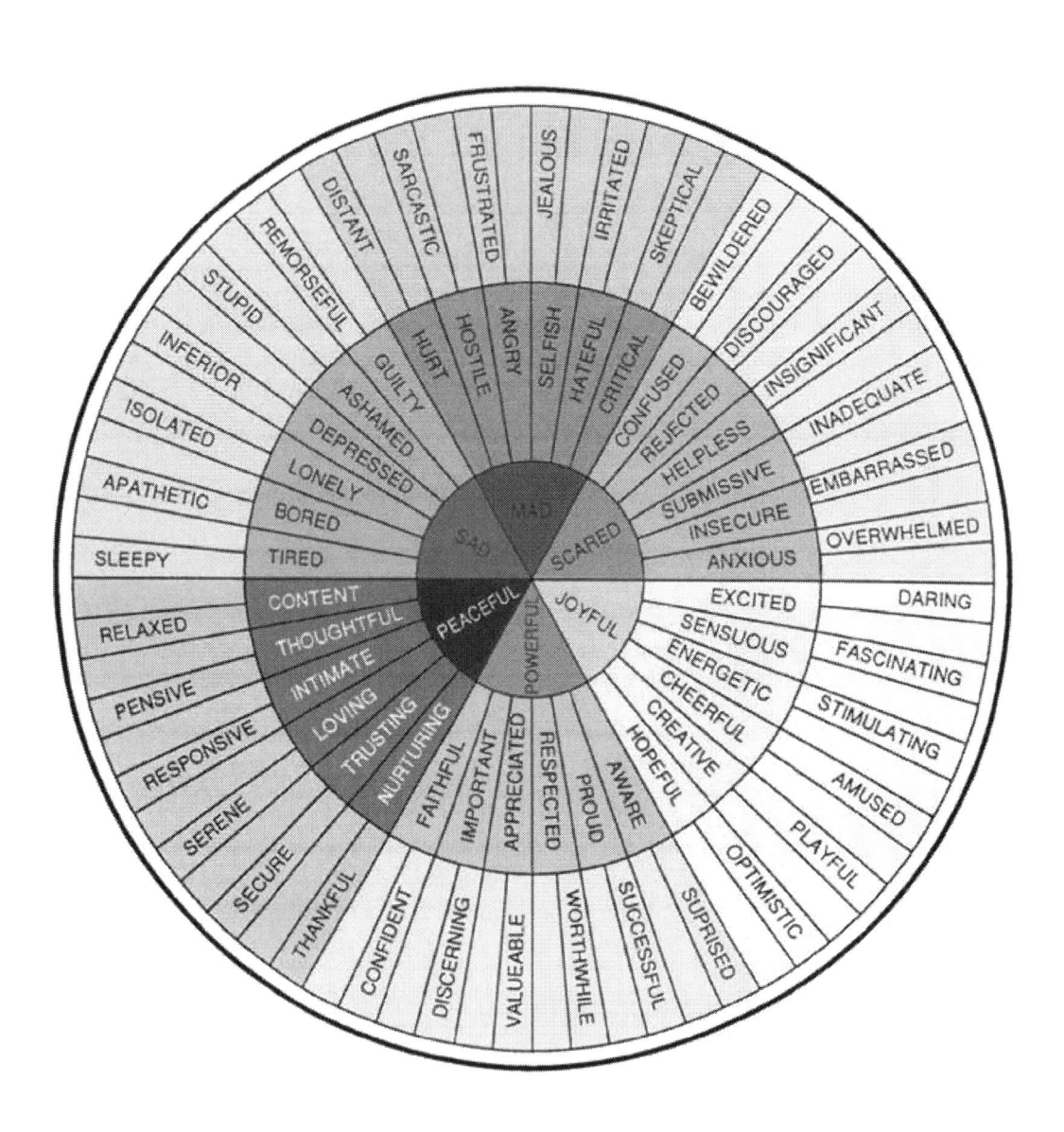

Appendix 2: Table of Virtues

Love	Joy	Peace	Patience	Kindness
Goodness	Gentleness	Faithfulness	Self-Control	Generosity
Justice	Temperance	Prudence	Fortitude	Honesty
Loyalty	Optimism	Endurance	Gratitude	Compassion
Honor	Sobriety	Friendship	Responsibility	Work
Courage	Perseverance	Faith	Hope	Humor
Song	Goodness	Serenity	Humility	Chastity
Delight	Contentment	Repentance	Frugality	Forgiveness
Duty	Enthusiasm	Gravity	Integrity	Self-Discipline
Empathy	Charity	Mercy	Strength	Wisdom
Service	Consistency	Innocence	Attention	Mildness

Further Resources

"Free Personality Test." Edited by Neris Analytics, *16Personalities*, 2011, www.16personalities.com/free-personality-test.

- This free personality test based off of the Myers-Briggs Type Indicator is a great introduction to how cognitive functions influence personality.

Goodman, Lion. "The Master List of Virtues." *The Master List of Virtues*, 2009, beliefcloset.com/wp-content/uploads/2010/05/Virtues-The-Master-List.pdf.

- A comprehensive list of words in English that indicate virtues, vices and values. It is an excellent resource for thinking about direction in personal growth.

Mendaglio, Sal. *Dabrowski's Theory of Positive Disintegration*. Great Potential Press, 2008.

- This collection of essays by students of Kazimierz Dabrowski is a very accessible introduction to the Theory of Positive Disintegration. It is not as highly technical as Dabrowski's own writing, but is a thorough treatment.

Pennock, Dee, and Sally Pierone. *Who Is God? Who Am I? Who Are You?* Greek Orthodox Archdiocese of America, 2005.

- Although geared towards teenagers, this clear-headed and profound book explores the intersections between spirituality and psychology in distilled and accessible language that people of all ages might find useful.

Stevens, Jane Ellen. "Got Your ACE Score?" *ACEs Too High*, 10 July 2018, acestoohigh.com/got-your-ace-score/.

- This article contains both the questions for Adverse Childhood Experiences (ACES) and Resiliency, as well as information from the CDC study on how ACES and resiliency can effect physical health.

Webber, Meletios. *Steps of Transformation: an Orthodox Priest Explores the Twelve Steps*. Conciliar Press, 2003.

- This book, spiritual in nature, is an excellent guide to understanding and using the Twelve Steps in one's personal development. Although the Twelve Steps were created for alcoholics, Webber's treatment demonstrates how the process can be beneficial for all of us.

Influences

Buber, Martin, and Walter Arnold Kaufmann. *I And Thou. / Martin Buber.* Simon & Schuster, 1970.

- This beautiful book of philosophy ponders the self and its relationship to others. There are two kinds of "I"—the "I-It" and the "I-You", and each of these "I's" has the potential to appear in our relationships with others, with ourselves, with the world around us, and with God.

Dabrowski, Kazimierz. *Positive Disintegration.* MAURICE BASSETT, 2018.

- A theory of personality development that describes five levels of personality, three factors that form our personalities, and the beneficial role of neurosis in personal development.

Larchet, Jean-Claude. *Therapy of Spiritual Illness.* Trans. Fr. Kilian Sprecher. Alexander Press, 2012.

- A comprehensive synthesis of the works of the Church fathers with the practical nature of spiritual healing and the development of undistorted selfhood.

Schwartz-Salant, Nathan. *The Mystery of Human Relationship: Alchemy and the Transformation of Self.* Routledge, 1998.

- An in-depth treatment of Jungian and alchemical symbolism in human relationships, this well-respected author has written numerous titles geared for professionals.

Made in the USA
Coppell, TX
27 May 2020